A
LIST

T0151819

Also by Margaret Atwood

Poetry

Fiction

Nonfiction

MARGARET ATWOOD

POWER POLITICS

POEMS

LIST

First published in 1971 by House of Anansi Press Ltd.
Revised edition published in 1996
This edition published in Canada and the USA in 2018 by House of Anansi Press Inc.
www.houseofanansi.com

House of Anansi Press is committed to protecting our natural environment.
This book is made of material from well-managed FSC®-certified forests and other
controlled sources.

House of Anansi Press is a Global Certified Accessible™ (GCA by Benetech) publisher.
The ebook version of this book meets stringent accessibility standards and is available
to students and readers with print disabilities.

25 24 23 22 21   3 4 5 6 7

Library and Archives Canada Cataloguing in Publication

Atwood, Margaret, 1939–, author
Power politics : poems / Margaret Atwood.

Previously published: Concord, Ontario: Anansi, 1996.
ISBN 978-1-4870-0455-2 (softcover)

I. Title.

PS8501.T86P6 2018   C811'.54   C2017-907401-6

Library of Congress Control Number: 2017961331

Series design: Brian Morgan
Cover illustration: Chloe Cushman
(After the first-edition cover by William Kimber)

*House of Anansi Press respectfully acknowledges that the land on which we operate is the
Traditional Territory of many Nations, including the Anishinabeg, the Wendat, and the
Haudenosaunee. It is also the Treaty Lands of the Mississaugas of the Credit.*

 Canada Council   Conseil des Arts
for the Arts   du Canada    ONTARIO ARTS COUNCIL
CONSEIL DES ARTS DE L'ONTARIO
an Ontario government agency
un organisme du gouvernement de l'Ontario

*We acknowledge for their financial support of our publishing program
the Canada Council for the Arts, the Ontario Arts Council, and the Government of Canada
through the Canada Book Fund.*

Printed and bound in Canada

MIX
Paper from
responsible sources
FSC® C103567

POWER POLITICS

INTRODUCTION
BY JAN ZWICKY

What, at this moment in the history of Europe and its post-colonial cultures, can be said with any degree of assurance about heterosexual politics? That they are inflamed. That polarization is occurring. That unprecedented anger is being expressed by women towards powerful males who have behaved in sexually abusive, corrupt, and exploitative ways. That many heterosexual men understand and sympathize with this anger, but are confused about what mores now obtain. That the most politically powerful man in the world, a man who is on videotape rhapsodizing about real or imagined sexual predation, remains securely in office. That due process is frequently scorned as an instrument of the oppressive order and that a new virtue is prescribed in its stead: faith in women's truthfulness. That social media have played a crucial role in the uprising. And, most importantly, that heterosexual relations appear to be undergoing a profound sea change. It is possible that we are on the cusp of a new Reformation.

The old Reformation, which consumed much of the sixteenth and seventeenth centuries in Europe, was concerned with ending corruption and abuses of power in the Catholic Church. Prior to the publication of Martin Luther's famous *Ninety-Five Theses*, there had been at least a century of protest focused on the sale of so-called indulgences, whereby the Church filled its coffers in return for the remission of sins. In 1517, Luther sent his *Ninety-Five Theses* disputing "the power and efficacy of indulgences" to his bishop. The *Theses* were originally published in Latin, but early in 1518 they were translated into German and, owing to the new technology of the printing press, within months copies had spread throughout Europe.

A key tenet of Luther's alternative view was that salvation was a gift from God, who couldn't be bought; it therefore could be achieved by faith alone, and did not require, indeed could not require, justification through good works. Among the most egregious offenders against genuine Christianity, according to Luther, was the pope himself — a Medici, and one of the richest men in Europe — who had instituted a sale of indulgences among the German poor to pay for the reconstruction of St. Peter's Basilica.

As the reformist view took hold, there were uprisings. By the mid-1520s monasteries, convents, episcopal palaces, and libraries were being destroyed. Luther condemned the mob, preaching the necessity of patience and calling for the exercise of canonical Christian virtues such as charity and faith in God's will to effect the necessary changes without violence. In 1545, however, a year before Luther's death, at the Council of Trent, the Church went on the offensive. It launched the Counter-Reformation, which spawned the French Wars of Religion, the Long Turkish War, massive witch hunts, and the terrifying violence of the Thirty Years' War, in which Germany is thought to have lost up to twenty percent of its population.

The achievements of the old Reformation were, in the end, mixed. The reformers succeeded in getting rid of indulgences, but they did so at the cost of splitting the Church. With hindsight, we can see that the Reformation's embrace of individualism and literacy allowed it to merge easily with the cultural ideals of the Scientific Revolution and the Enlightenment. The Reformation marks the end of Medieval culture in Europe and the transition to a new order whose apotheosis is secular technocracy. There is a direct line from Luther's actions in 1517 to Nietzsche's pronouncement of God's death in 1882.

Although there are several parallels between the old Reformation and the new one (the most intriguing of which, to my mind, is the role of communications technologies), there are several crucial discontinuities. One is the absence, in the present era, of a single figure like Luther around whom the *declaration* of a new order has crystallized. Discontent among women is millennia, not decades, old; famous voices of opposition number in the hundreds not handfuls. And the matter at issue is sexual, not religious, mores. Sex, it has been argued, is a less malleable feature of human existence than spiritual belief, and we ought, therefore, to expect sexual behaviours to be less open to variation. Estrogen and testosterone are psychotropic drugs but—unlike wine, peyote, and magic mushrooms—their use is not yet wholly optional for most members of most societies. It is, however, now technologically possible to alter one's sex. Or eliminate it. Is sex, then, set to go the way of religion? That might be one projection we should take seriously if we wish to learn from the lessons of the old Reformation.

Into this charged atmosphere comes Anansi's reissue of Margaret Atwood's 1971 collection *Power Politics*. Atwood has said that *The Edible Woman*, the novel published just before *Power Politics*, was not written in response to the rise of feminist consciousness in North America. I believe the same is true of *Power Politics*. The book is not a manifesto, it is a personal testament. It does not tell us that the personal is political, it shows that this is so. There is a power to such showing that slogans cannot touch and statistics cannot match.

Atwood herself characterizes the book as a "non-sonnet sequence." Why not just say "sequence" when the poems don't have anything like fourteen lines? Partly because sonnet sequences, in their heyday, were typically concerned with love. The narrative arc in Petrarch and Sidney follows the tradition of courtly love: an intense passion for an unavailable person is transmuted into love of God. Not so in *Power Politics*. But in its preoccupation with disintegrating love, it has one famous recent predecessor: George Meredith's sonnet sequence *Modern Love*. And it is perhaps worth remembering that in her school days, Atwood was a Victorianist.

The other reason it can be helpful to think of *Power Politics* as a non-sonnet sequence has to do with the texture of its thought, a delight in linguistic intelligence that we associate with the flowering of the English sonnet in the Elizabethan era. Although Marvell was not particularly a sonneteer, he shared a sensibility with those who developed the form. Eliot's observations on his wit are especially pertinent here:

> Wit is not erudition.... It is not cynicism, though it has a kind of toughness which may be confused with cynicism by the tender-minded. It is confused with erudition because it belongs to an educated mind, rich in generations of experience; and it is confused with cynicism because it implies a constant inspection and criticism of experience.

I can think of few more apt descriptions of *Power Politics*: a relentless inspection and criticism of experience by an educated mind. Chief among its virtues is its combination of precision and complexity: the ambiguities are crystal clear. Its testimony is highly nuanced—there is sorrow and bewilderment as well as anger—but there is little confusion and absolutely no hand-wringing. Despite the suffering it documents, the gaze remains steady, a steadiness that gleams in the pointed beauty of the language. There are, not infrequently, elegant jokes.

One of *Power Politics'* intricately etched ambiguities is the speaker's role in the failing relationship. Various oppressive stereotypes haunt the poems—romantic images of women waiting for their men to return from hunting or from war, the male as Bluebeard or as military commander, wooden, insulated from reality, his tongue scarring the mildewed flowers. But the speaker also understands that she is complicit in maintaining the relationship.

I can't tell you I don't want you
the sea is on your side

You have the earth's nets
I have only a pair of scissors.

. . .

Putting on my clothes
again, retreating, closing doors
I am amazed / I can continue
to think, eat, anything

How can I stop you

Why did I create you

(Few more potent uses of the slash than in "I am amazed /
I can continue"!) And the speaker also recognizes that she is
complicit in the relationship's demise.

We are hard on each other
and call it honesty, . . .
The things we say are
true; it is our crooked
aims, our choices
turn them criminal.

She understands that it is she, not her lover, who is distant,
analytical, the exploiter of his pain for her professional
advancement, the agent of his crucifixion. This is what power
politics do: they force all parties to assume the stance of
antagonist. Their root is territoriality.

   In creating the cover image for this new edition, illustrator
Chloe Cushman took her cue from the cover image on the

first edition. The original cover was designed by William Kimber, but the image was drawn to Atwood's specifications. It shows a bandaged female figure suspended by the foot from the extended gauntlet of a fully armoured knight. (Is the armour shining? Hard to tell, but it's a reasonable bet.) The figure of the suspended woman is a clear echo of the Hanged Man in the tarot deck: her arms are akimbo, hands behind her back; her free leg (her right, though, not the Hanged Man's left) is crossed behind the leg from which she hangs; her gaze is clear and direct, her expression mild. In the tarot, the Hanged Man is a card of potent and paradoxical transformation: it is the image of dying to an old order so that one may be carried beyond it, of surrendering to the necessity of profound change while suspending action.

It is, thus, a card complementary to the Wheel of Fortune, another image in which Atwood has expressed deep interest. In the old fifteenth-century decks, she notes, the Wheel of Fortune shows folks who've previously had good luck getting thrown off or pulled under and crushed, and those who haven't previously been lucky being elevated to favour. If you get this card, check your privilege. Things may look good now, but they probably won't tomorrow. It is a particularly dark card because although those on top and those on the bottom are constantly changing position, the structure of change remains superficial. There's no way forward to a better arrangement for all.

The Hanged Man, by contrast, presages deep realignment. The image was based on a particularly gruesome Italian punishment for traitors. But a traitor to what or to whom? If you draw the Hanged Man, you are at a crossroads. You need to break with some pattern of behaviour to which you are committed, but you will not succeed simply by bashing away at what is restricting you. The last poem in the book reads:

1

You walk towards me
carrying a new death
which is mine and no-one else's;

Your face is silver
and flat, scaled like a fish

The death you bring me
is curved, it is the shape
of doorknobs, moons
glass paperweights

Inside it, snow and lethal
flakes of gold fall endlessly
over an ornamental scene,
a man and a woman, hands joined and running

2

Nothing I can do will slow you
down, nothing
will make you arrive any sooner

You are serious, a gift-bearer,
you set one foot
in front of the other

through the weeks and months, across
the rocks, up from
the pits and starless
deep nights of the sea

towards firm ground and safety.

The Hanged Man is also regarded as an image of exceptional spiritual attainment: wisdom that sees things for what they really are.

What might the Hanged Woman offer readers in this turbulent time—readers who recognize their own tortured experience in hers, and readers with whom she is bound in antagonistic struggle? The long view, perhaps, coupled with a steadfast commitment to justice. A wish to change the structure of the old order, not just to reverse who's on top and who's on bottom. A commitment to the honesty that underlies genuine justice, to seeing ourselves and our complicities for what they are. And patience: a brake on knee-jerk desires for vengeance. Faith in the goodness of others. Hope. Charity.

Heriot Ridge
13 January 2018

JAN ZWICKY has published more than a dozen books of poetry and prose, including *The Long Walk, Wisdom & Metaphor,* and *Songs for Relinquishing the Earth.* She lives on Quadra Island, off the west coast of British Columbia.

POWER POLITICS

you fit into me
like a hook into an eye

a fish hook
an open eye

⊛ He reappears

You rose from a snowbank
with three heads, all
your hands were in your pockets

I said, haven't
I seen you somewhere before

You pretended you were hungry
I offered you sandwiches and gingerale
but you refused

Your six eyes glowed
red, you shivered cunningly

Can't we
be friends I said;
you didn't answer.

You take my hand and
I'm suddenly in a bad movie,
it goes on and on and
why am I fascinated

We waltz in slow motion
through an air stale with aphorisms
we meet behind endless potted palms
you climb through the wrong windows

Other people are leaving
but I always stay till the end
I paid my money, I
want to see what happens.

In chance bathtubs I have to
peel you off me
in the form of smoke and melted
celluloid

       Have to face it I'm
finally an addict,
the smell of popcorn and worn plush
lingers for weeks

She considers evading him

I can change my-
self more easily
than I can change you

I could grow bark and
become a shrub

or switch back in time
to the woman image left
in cave rubble, the drowned
stomach bulbed with fertility,
face a tiny bead, a
lump, queen of the termites

or (better) speed myself up,
disguise myself in the knuckles
and purple-veined veils of old ladies,
become arthritic and genteel

or one twist further:
collapse across your
bed clutching my heart
and pull the nostalgic sheet up over
my waxed farewell smile

which would be inconvenient
but final.

❀ *They eat out*

In restaurants we argue
over which of us will pay for your funeral

though the real question is
whether or not I will make you immortal.

At the moment only I
can do it and so

I raise the magic fork
over the plate of beef fried rice

and plunge it into your heart.
There is a faint pop, a sizzle

and through your own split head
you rise up glowing;

the ceiling opens
a voice sings Love Is A Many

Splendoured Thing
you hang suspended above the city

in blue tights and a red cape,
your eyes flashing in unison.

The other diners regard you
some with awe, some only with boredom:

they cannot decide if you are a new weapon
or only a new advertisement.

As for me, I continue eating;
I liked you better the way you were,
but you were always ambitious.

After the agony in the guest
bedroom, you lying by the
overturned bed
your face uplifted, neck propped
against the windowsill, my arm
under you, cold moon
shining down through the window

wine mist rising
around you, an almost-
visible halo

You say, Do you
love me, do you love me

I answer you:
I stretch your arms out
one to either side,
your head slumps forward.

Later I take you home
in a taxi, and you
are sick in the bathtub.

My beautiful wooden leader
with your heartful of medals
made of wood, fixing it
each time so you almost win,

you long to be bandaged
before you have been cut.
My love for you is the love
of one statue for another: tensed

and static. General, you enlist
my body in your heroic
struggle to become real:
though you promise bronze rescues

you hold me by the left ankle
so that my head brushes the ground,
my eyes are blinded,
my hair fills with white ribbons.

There are hordes of me now, alike
and paralyzed, we follow you
scattering floral tributes
under your hooves.

Magnificent on your wooden horse
you point with your fringed hand;
the sun sets, and the people all
ride off in the other direction.

✺ *He is a strange biological phenomenon*

Like eggs and snails you have a shell

You are widespread
and bad for the garden,
hard to eradicate

Scavenger, you feed
only on dead meat:

Your flesh by now
is pure protein,
smooth as gelatin
or the slick bellies of leeches

You are sinuous and without bones
Your tongue leaves tiny scars
the ashy texture of mildewed flowers

You thrive on smoke; you have
no chlorophyll; you move
from place to place like a disease

Like mushrooms you live in closets
and come out only at night.

You want to go back
to where the sky was inside us

animals ran through us, our hands
blessed and killed according to our
wisdom, death
made real blood come out

But face it, we have been
improved, our heads float
several inches above our necks
moored to us by
rubber tubes and filled with
clever bubbles,

        our bodies
are populated with billions
of soft pink numbers
multiplying and analyzing
themselves, perfecting
their own demands, no trouble to anyone.

I love you by
sections and when you work.

Do you want to be illiterate?
This is the way it is, get used to it.

✾ *Their attitudes differ*

1

To understand
each other: anything
but that, & to avoid it

I will suspend my search for
germs if you will keep
your fingers off the microfilm
hidden inside my skin

2

I approach this love
like a biologist
pulling on my rubber
gloves & white labcoat

You flee from it
like an escaped political
prisoner, and no wonder

3

You held out your hand
I took your fingerprints

You asked for love
I gave you only descriptions

Please die I said
so I can write about it

They travel by air

A different room, this month
a worse one, where your
body with head
attached and my head with
body attached coincide briefly

I want questions and you want
only answers, but the building
is warming up, there is not much

time and time is not
fast enough for us any
more, the building sweeps
away, we are off course, we
separate, we hurtle towards each other
at the speed of sound, everything roars

we collide sightlessly and
fall, the pieces of us
mixed as disaster
and hit the pavement of this room
in a blur of silver fragments

not the shore but an aquarium
filled with exhausted water and warm
seaweed
       glass clouded
with dust and algae
             tray
with the remains of dinner

smells of salt carcasses and uneaten shells

sunheat comes from wall
grating   no breeze

you sprawl across
            the bed like a marooned
starfish
        you are sand-
coloured
      on my back

your hand floats belly up

You have made your escape,
your known addresses
crumple in the wind, the city
unfreezes with relief

traffic shifts back
to its routines, the swollen
buildings return to

normal, I walk believably
from house to store, nothing

remembers you but the bruises
on my thighs and the inside of my skull.

Because you are never here
but always there, I forget
not you but what you look like

You drift down the street
in the rain, your face
dissolving, changing shape, the colours
running together

My walls absorb
you, breathe you forth
again, you resume
yourself, I do not recognize you

You rest on the bed
watching me watching
you, we will never know
each other any better

than we do now

Imperialist, keep off
the trees I said.

No use: you walk backwards,
admiring your own footprints.

After all you are quite
ordinary: 2 arms 2 legs
a head, a reasonable
body, toes & fingers, a few
eccentricities, a few honesties
but not too many, too many
postponements & regrets but

you'll adjust to it, meeting
deadlines and other
people, pretending to love
the wrong woman some of the
time, listening to your brain
shrink, your diaries
expanding as you grow older,

growing older, of course you'll
die but not yet, you'll outlive
even my distortions of you

and there isn't anything
I want to do about the fact
that you are unhappy & sick

you aren't sick & unhappy
only alive & stuck with it.

Small tactics

1

These days my fingers bleed
even before I bite them

Can't play it safe, can't play
at all any more

Let's go back please
to the games, they were
more fun and less painful

2

You too have your gentle
moments, you too have
eyelashes, each of your eyes
is a different colour

in the half light
your body stutters against
me, tentative as moths, your
skin is nervous

                I touch
your mouth, I don't
want to hurt
you any more
now than I have to

3

Waiting for news of you
which does not come, I have to
guess you

       You are
in the city, climbing the stairs
already, that is you at the door

or you have gone, your last
message to me left
illegible on the mountain
road, quick
scribble of glass and blood

4

For stones, opening
is not easy

Staying closed is
less pain but

your anger finally
is more dangerous

To be picked up and thrown
(you won't stop) against

the ground, picked up
and thrown again and again

5

It's getting bad, you weren't
there again

Wire silences, you trying

to think of something you haven't
said, at least to me

Me trying to give
the impression it isn't

getting bad   at least
not yet

6

I walk the cell, open the window,
shut the window, the little
motors click
and whir, I turn on all the
taps and switches

I take pills, I drink water, I kneel

O electric lights
that shine on my suitcases and my fears

Let me stop caring
about anything but skinless
wheels and smoothly-
running money

Get me out of this trap, this
body, let me be
like you, closed and useful

7

What do you expect after this?
Applause? Your name on stone?

You will have nothing
but me and in a worse way than before,

my face packed in cotton
in a white gift box, the features

dissolving and re-forming so quickly
I seem only to flicker.

There are better ways of doing this

It would be so good if you'd
only stay up there
where I put you, I could
believe, you'd solve
most of my religious problems

you have to admit it's easier
when you're somewhere else

but today it's this
deserted mattress, music over-
heard through the end wall, you giving me
a hard time again for the fun
of it or just for

the publicity, when we leave each other
it will be so
we can say we did.

yes at first you
go down smooth as
pills, all of me
breathes you in and then it's

a kick in the head, orange
and brutal, sharp jewels
hit and my
hair splinters

        the adjectives
fall away from me, no
threads left holding
me, I flake apart
layer by
layer down
quietly to the bone, my skull
unfolds to an astounded flower

regrowing the body, learning
speech again takes
days and longer
each time / too much of
this is fatal

The accident has occurred,
the ship has broken, the motor
of the car has failed, we have been
separated from the others,
we are alone in the sand, the ocean,
the frozen snow

I remember what I have to do
in order to stay alive,
I take stock of our belongings
most of them useless

I know I should be digging shelters,
killing seabirds and making
clothes from their feathers,
cutting the rinds from cacti, chewing
roots for water, scraping through
the ice for treebark, for moss

but I rest here without power
to save myself, tasting
salt in my mouth, the fact that
you won't save me

watching the mirage of us
hands locked, smiling,
as it fades into the white desert.

I touch you, straighten the sheet, you turn over
in the bed, tender
sun comes through the curtains

Which of us will survive
which of us will survive the other

1

We are hard on each other
and call it honesty,
choosing our jagged truths
with care and aiming them across
the neutral table.

The things we say are
true; it is our crooked
aims, our choices
turn them criminal.

2

Of course your lies
are more amusing:
you make them new each time.

Your truths, painful and boring
repeat themselves over & over
perhaps because you own
so few of them

3

A truth should exist,
it should not be used
like this. If I love you

is that a fact or a weapon?

4

Does the body lie
moving like this, are these
touches, hairs, wet
soft marble my tongue runs over
lies you are telling me?

Your body is not a word,
it does not lie or
speak truth either.

It is only
here or not here.

He shifts from east to west

Because we have no history
I construct one for you

making use of what
there is, parts of other people's
lives, paragraphs
I invent, now and then
an object, a watch, a picture
you claim as yours

(What did go on in that red
brick building with the fire
escape? Which river?)

(You said you took
the boat, you forget too much.)

I locate you on streets, in cities
I've never seen, you walk
against a background crowded
with lifelike detail

which crumbles and turns grey
when I look too closely.

Why should I need
to explain you, perhaps
this is the right place for you

The mountains in this hard
clear vacancy are blue tin
edges, you appear
without prelude midway between
my eyes and the nearest trees,

your colours bright, your
outline flattened

suspended in the air with no more
reason for occurring
exactly here than this billboard,
this highway or that cloud.

At first I was given centuries
to wait in caves, in leather
tents, knowing you would never come back

Then it speeded up: only
several years between
the day you jangled off
into the mountains, and the day (it was
spring again) I rose from the embroidery
frame at the messenger's entrance.

That happened twice, or was it
more; and there was once, not so
long ago, you failed,
and came back in a wheelchair
with a moustache and a sunburn
and were insufferable.

Time before last though, I remember
I had a good eight months between
running alongside the train, skirts hitched, handing
you violets in at the window
and opening the letter; I watched
your snapshot fade for twenty years.

And last time (I drove to the airport
still dressed in my factory
overalls, the wrench
I had forgotten sticking out of the back
pocket; there you were,
zippered and helmeted, it was zero
hour, you said Be
Brave) it was at least three weeks before
I got the telegram and could start regretting.

But recently, the bad evenings
there are only seconds
between the warning on the radio and the
explosion; my hands
don't reach you

and on quieter nights
you jump up from
your chair without even touching your dinner
and I can scarcely kiss you goodbye
before you run out into the street and they shoot

You refuse to own
yourself, you permit
others to do it for you:

you become slowly more public,
in a year there will be nothing left
of you but a megaphone

or you will descend through the roof
with the spurious authority of a
government official,
blue as a policeman, grey as a used angel,
having long forgotten the difference
between an annunciation and a parking ticket

or you will be slipped under
the door, your skin furred with cancelled
airmail stamps, your kiss no longer literature
but fine print, a set of instructions.

If you deny these uniforms
and choose to repossess
yourself, your future

will be less dignified, more painful, death will be sooner,
(it is no longer possible
to be both human and alive): lying piled with
the others, your face and body
covered so thickly with scars
only the eyes show through.

We hear nothing these days
from the ones in power

Why talk when you are a shoulder
or a vault

Why talk when you are
helmeted with numbers

Fists have many forms;
a fist knows what it can do

without the nuisance of speaking:
it grabs and smashes.

From those inside or under
words gush like toothpaste.

Language, the fist
proclaims by squeezing
is for the weak only.

You did it
it was you who started the countdown

and you conversely
on whom the demonic number
zero descended in the form of an egg-
bodied machine
coming at you like a
football or a bloated thumb

and it was you whose skin
fell off bubbling
all at once when the fence
accidentally touched you

and you also who laughed
when you saw it happen.

When will you learn
the flame and the wood / flesh
it burns are whole and the same?

You attempt merely power
you accomplish merely suffering

How long do you expect me to wait
while you cauterize your
senses, one
after another
turning yourself to an
impervious glass tower?

How long will you demand I love you?

I'm through, I won't make
any more flowers for you

I judge you as the trees do
by dying

your back is rough all
over like a cat's tongue / I stroke
you lightly and you shiver

you clench yourself, withhold
even your flesh
outline / pleasure is what
you take but will not accept.

believe me, allow
me to touch you
gently, it may be the last

time / your closed eyes beat
against my fingers
I slip my hand down
your neck, rest on the pulse

you pull away

there is something in your throat that wants
to get out and you won't let it.

This is a mistake,
these arms and legs
that don't work any more

Now it's broken
and no space for excuses.

The earth doesn't comfort,
it only covers up
if you have the decency to stay quiet

The sun doesn't forgive,
it looks and keeps going.

Night seeps into us
through the accidents we have
inflicted on each other

Next time we commit
love, we ought to
choose in advance what to kill.

Beyond truth,
tenacity: of those
dwarf trees & mosses,
hooked into straight rock
believing the sun's lies & thus
refuting / gravity

& of this cactus, gathering
itself together
against the sand, yes tough
rind & spikes but doing
the best it can

They are hostile nations

1

In view of the fading animals
the proliferation of sewers and fears
the sea clogging, the air
nearing extinction

we should be kind, we should
take warning, we should forgive each other

Instead we are opposite, we
touch as though attacking,

the gifts we bring
even in good faith maybe
warp in our hands to
implements, to manoeuvres

2

Put down the target of me
you guard inside your binoculars,
in turn I will surrender

this aerial photograph
(your vulnerable
sections marked in red)
I have found so useful

See, we are alone in
the dormant field, the snow
that cannot be eaten or captured

3

Here there are no armies
here there is no money

It is cold and getting colder

We need each others'
breathing, warmth, surviving
is the only war
we can afford, stay

walking with me, there is almost
time / if we can only
make it as far as

the (possibly) last summer

Returning from the dead
used to be something I did well

I began asking why
I began forgetting how

Spring again, can I stand it
shooting its needles into
the earth, my head, both
used to darkness

Snow on brown soil and
the squashed caterpillar
coloured liquid lawn

Winter collapses
in slack folds around
my feet / no leaves yet / loose fat

Thick lilac buds crouch for the
spurt but I
hold back

Not ready / help me
what I want from you is
moonlight smooth as
wind, long hairs of water

This year I intended children
a space where I could raise
foxes and strawberries, finally
be reconciled to fur seeds & burrows

but the entrails of dead cards
are against me, foretell
it will be water, the

element that shaped
me, that I shape by
being in

      It is the blue
cup, I fill it

it is the pond again
where the children, looking from
the side of the boat, see their mother

upside down, lifesize, hair streaming
over the slashed throat
and words fertilize each other
in the cold and with bulging eyes

I am sitting on the
edge of the impartial
bed, I have been turned to crystal, you enter

bringing love in the form of
a cardboard box (empty)
a pocket (empty)
some hands (also empty)

Be careful I say but
how can you
              the empty
thing comes out of your hands, it
fills the room slowly, it is
a pressure, a lack of
pressure
              Like a deep sea
creature with glass bones and wafer
eyes drawn
to the surface, I break

open, the pieces of me
shine briefly in your empty hands

I see you fugitive, stumbling across the prairie,
lungs knotted by thirst, sunheat
nailing you down, all the things
after you that can be after you
with their clamps and poisoned mazes

Should I help you?
Should I make you a mirage?

My right hand unfolds rivers
around you, my left hand releases its trees,
I speak rain,
I spin you a night and you hide in it.

Now you have one enemy
instead of many.

We are standing facing each other
in an eighteenth century room
with fragile tables and mirrors
in carved frames; the curtains,
red brocade, are drawn

the doors are shut, you aren't talking,
the chandeliers aren't talking, the carpets

also remain silent.
You stay closed, your skin
is buttoned firmly around you,
your mouth is a tin decoration,
you are in the worst possible taste.

You are fake as the marble trim
around the fireplace, there is nothing
I wouldn't do to be away
from here.   I do nothing

because the light changes, the tables
and mirrors radiate from around you,
you step backwards away from me
the length of the room

holding cupped in your hands
behind your back
                        an offering
a gold word   a signal

I need more than
air, blood, it would open
everything

which you won't let me see.

Sleeping in sun-
light (you occupy
me so completely

run through my brain as warm
chemicals and melted
gold, spread out wings to the
ends of my fingers
reach my heart and
stop, digging your claws in

If a bird what kind /
nothing I have ever
seen in air / you fly
through earth and water casting
a red shadow

The door wakes me, this is
your jewelled reptilian
eye in darkness next to
mine, shining feathers of
hair sift over my forehead

What is it, it does not
move like love, it does
not want to know, it
does not want to stroke, unfold

it does not even want to
touch, it is more like
an animal (not
loving) a
thing trapped, you move
wounded, you are hurt, you hurt,
you want to get out, you want
to tear yourself out, I am

the outside, I am snow and
space, pathways, you gather
yourself, your muscles

clutch, you move
into me as though I
am (wrenching
your way through, this is
urgent, it is your
life) the
last chance for freedom

You are the sun
in reverse, all energy
flows into you and is
abolished; you refuse
houses, you smell of
catastrophe, I see you
blind and one-handed, flashing
in the dark, trees breaking
under your feet, you demand,
you demand

I lie mutilated beside
you; beneath us there are
sirens, fires, the people run
squealing, the city
is crushed and gutted,
the ends of your fingers bleed
from 1000 murders

Putting on my clothes
again, retreating, closing doors
I am amazed / I can continue
to think, eat, anything

How can I stop you

Why did I create you

Hesitations outside the door

1

I'm telling the wrong lies,
they are not even useful.

The right lies would at least
be keys, they would open the door.

The door is closed; the chairs,
the tables, the steel bowl, myself

shaping bread in the kitchen, wait
outside it.

2

That was a lie also,
I could go in if I wanted to.

Whose house is this
we both live in
but neither of us owns

How can I be expected
to find my way around

I could go in if I wanted to,
that's not the point, I don't have time,

I should be doing something
other than you.

3

What do you want from me
you who walk towards me over the long floor

your arms outstretched, your heart
luminous through the ribs

around your head a crown
of shining blood

This is your castle, this is your metal door,
these are your stairs, your

bones, you twist all possible
dimensions into your own

4

Alternate version: you advance
through the grey streets of this house,

the walls crumble, the dishes
thaw, vines grow
on the softening refrigerator

I say, leave me
alone, this is my winter,

I will stay here if I choose

You will not listen
to resistances, you cover me

with flags, a dark red
season, you delete from me
all other colours

5

Don't let me do this to you,
you are not those other people,
you are yourself

Take off the signatures, the false
bodies, this love
which does not fit you

This is not a house, there are no doors,
get out while it is
open, while you still can

6

If we make stories for each other
about what is in the room
we will never have to go in.

You say: my other wives
are in there, they are all
beautiful and happy, they love me, why
disturb them

I say: it is only
a cupboard, my collection
of envelopes, my painted
eggs, my rings

In your pockets the thin women
hang on their hooks, dismembered

Around my neck I wear
the head of the beloved, pressed
in the metal retina like a picked flower.

7

Should we go into it
together / If I go into it
with you I will never come out

If I wait outside I can salvage
this house or what is left
of it, I can keep
my candles, my dead uncles
my restrictions

but you will go
alone, either
way is loss

Tell me what it is for

In the room we will find nothing
In the room we will find each other

Lying here, everything in me
brittle and pushing you away

This is not something I
wanted, I tell you

silently, not admitting
the truth of where

I am, so far
up, the sky incredible and dark

blue, each breath
a gift in the steep air

How hard even the boulders
find it to grow here

and I don't know how to accept
your freedom, I don't know

what to do with this
precipice, this joy

What do you see, I ask / my voice
absorbed by stone and outer

space / you are asleep, you see
what there is. Beside you

I bend and enter

I look up, you are standing
on the other side of the window

now   your body
glimmers in the dark

room / you rise above me
smooth, chill, stone-

white / you smell of tunnels
you smell of too much time

I should have used leaves
and silver to prevent you

instead I summoned

you are not a bird you do not fly
you are not an animal you do not run

you are not a man

your mouth is nothingness
where it touches me I vanish

you descend on me like age
you descend on me like earth

I can't tell you my name:
you don't believe I have one

I can't warn you this boat is falling
you planned it that way

You've never had a face
but you know that appeals to me

You are old enough to be my
skeleton: you know that also.

I can't tell you I don't want you
the sea is on your side

You have the earth's nets
I have only a pair of scissors.

When I look for you I find
water or moving shadow

There is no way I can lose you
when you are lost already.

They were all inaccurate:

the hinged bronze man, the fragile man
built of glass pebbles,
the fanged man with his opulent capes and boots

peeling away from you in scales.

It was my fault but you helped,
you enjoyed it.

Neither of us will enjoy
the rest: you following me
down streets, hallways, melting
when I touch you,
avoiding the sleeves of the bargains
I hold out for you,
your face corroded by truth,

crippled, persistent. You ask
like the wind, again and again and
wordlessly, for the one forbidden thing:

love without mirrors and not for
my reasons but your own.

He is last seen

1

You walk towards me
carrying a new death
which is mine and no-one else's;

Your face is silver
and flat, scaled like a fish

The death you bring me
is curved, it is the shape
of doorknobs, moons
glass paperweights

Inside it, snow and lethal
flakes of gold fall endlessly
over an ornamental scene,
a man and woman, hands joined and running

2

Nothing I can do will slow you
down, nothing
will make you arrive any sooner

You are serious, a gift-bearer,
you set one foot
in front of the other

through the weeks and months, across
the rocks, up from
the pits and starless
deep nights of the sea

towards firm ground and safety.

MARGARET ATWOOD is the author of more than forty-five books of fiction, poetry, and critical essays. Her most recent books include *Hag-Seed*, a novel revisitation of Shakespeare's play *The Tempest*, and *Angel Catbird*—featuring a cat-bird superhero—a graphic novel with co-creator Johnnie Christmas. She is a two-time winner of the Governor General's Literary Award, has won the Man Booker Award, and was inducted into Canada's Walk of Fame. Recently, her novel *The Handmaid's Tale* was adapted for television to international acclaim, and *Alias Grace* was made into a CBC mini-series by director and actor Sarah Polley. Margaret Atwood lives in Toronto with writer Graeme Gibson.

LIST

The A List